Lesley Anne Leach

cookies

simple and delicious easy-to-make recipes

This is a Parragon Publishing Book
This edition published in 2004

Parragon Publishing
Queen Street House
4 Queen Street
Bath BA1 1HE
United Kingdom

Copyright © Parragon 2001

ISBN: 1-40543-859-2

Printed in China

Produced by
THE BRIDGEWATER BOOK COMPANY LTD

Creative Director Terry Jeavons
Art Director Sarah Howerd
Editorial Director Fiona Biggs
Senior Editor Mark Truman
Editorial Assistants Simon Bailey, Tom Kitch
Photographer Trevor Leak
Home Economist Marianne Lumb
Page Make-up Chris and Jane Lanaway

COVER
Photographer Mark Wood
Home Economist Pamela Gwyther

NOTES FOR THE READER

- This book uses both imperial and metric measurements. Follow the same units of measurement throughout; do not mix imperial and metric.

- All spoon measurements are level: teaspoons are assumed to be 5 ml, and tablespoons are assumed to be 15 ml.

- Unless otherwise stated, milk is assumed to be whole and eggs are assumed to be medium.

- Recipes using raw or very lightly cooked eggs should be avoided by infants, the elderly, pregnant women, convalescents, and anyone suffering from an illness.

- Optional ingredients, variations or serving suggestions have not been included in the calculations. The times given are an approximate guide only. Preparation times differ according to the techniques used by different people and the cooking times vary as a result of the type of oven used.

contents

introduction

Cookies offer a sweet treat at any time of day and brighten up any special occasion. So, whether it's a chocolate brownie or an oat cookie for a coffee break, a fruit and nut cookie with a bedtime glass of milk, or a special heart-shaped surprise for your loved one on St. Valentine's Day, there are so many cookies to choose from that you'll find the right recipe to suit your taste buds any time.

All the recipes in this book are easy, but some are very easy and others are extremely easy-so there's no excuse to put off making some mouthwatering cookies straight away, whatever your level of culinary expertise.

Children love cookies, so why not get them to join in the baking fun (under careful supervision, of course)? They love making and baking cookies - particularly getting covered in flour and sampling mixture as they go, rolling

chocolate temptations
page 16

hazelnut & almond oaties
page 36

out dough and making interesting cookie shapes. Cookie-making is fun for children of all ages.

There's a cookie to suit every taste in this book. Whether you're a chocoholic, an oat cookie lover, a fruit 'n' nut fan, or you're having a party for the kids or celebrating a special occasion, you'll find a delicious recipe to add a little sweetness to your day.

easy

Recipes are graded as follows:
1 spoon = easy;
2 spoons = very easy;
3 spoons = extremely easy.

makes 24 cookies

Recipes make between 20 and 56 cookies. Simply halve the ingredient quantities to make half the number of cookies; do not mix imperial and metric measurements.

10 minutes

Preparation time. Where chilling the cookie dough is involved, this time has been added on separately.

10 minutes

Cooking time.

cherry & walnut cookies
page 62

snowy chocolate crispies
page 80

Chocolate has to be one of life's most tantalizing treats, as chocoholics everywhere would surely testify. In this section of mouthwatering cookies, you'll find cookies cooked with, covered in, or dipped in delicious chocolate of all kinds. The recipes here range from the children's favorite Chocolate Peanut Cookies to the sheer delightful self-indulgence of Chocolate Temptations–something for everyone.

chocolate cookies

chocolate & apple oaties

very easy   makes 24
cookies

15 minutes   10 minutes

ingredients

½ cup butter or margarine,
  plus extra for greasing
⅔ cup apple sauce
2 tbsp apple juice
½ cup raw brown sugar
1 tsp baking soda
1 tsp almond extract

¼ cup boiling water
1⅓ cups rolled oats
2 cups all-purpose flour, unsifted
pinch of salt
⅓ cup semisweet chocolate chips

Preheat the oven to 400°F/200°C. Grease a large cookie sheet.

Blend the apple sauce, apple juice, butter (or margarine), and sugar in a food processor until a fluffy consistency is reached.

In a separate bowl, mix together the baking soda, almond extract, and water, then add to the food processor and mix with the apple mixture. In another bowl, mix together the oats, flour, and salt, then gradually stir into the apple mixture and beat well. Stir in the chocolate chips.

Put 24 rounded tablespoonfuls of mixture onto the cookie sheet, ensuring that they are well spaced. Transfer to the preheated oven and bake for 15 minutes, or until the cookies are golden brown.

Remove the cookies from the oven, then transfer to a wire rack and let them cool completely before serving.

light & dark chocolate cookies

extremely easy | makes 24 cookies

10 minutes | 10–12 minutes

ingredients

½ cup butter or margarine,
  plus extra for greasing
scant ⅔ cup raw brown sugar
1 egg
1 tbsp corn syrup
1 tbsp water
1 tsp vanilla extract
½ tsp almond extract

generous 1 cup all-purpose flour, unsifted
½ tsp baking soda
pinch of salt
2 tbsp boiling water
1 cup rolled oats
½ cup semisweet chocolate chips
½ cup white chocolate chips

Preheat the oven to 350°F/180°C. Grease two large cookie sheets.

Put the butter (or margarine, if using), sugar, eggs, corn syrup, water, and vanilla and almond extract in a large bowl and beat together thoroughly.

In a separate bowl, mix together the flour, baking soda, salt, boiling water, and oats, and then add to the egg mixture. Beat together thoroughly.

Stir in the chocolate chips, then put rounded teaspoonfuls of the mixture onto the greased cookie sheets, ensuring that they are well spaced because they expand during cooking. You may need to make two batches of cookies. Transfer to the preheated oven and bake for 10–12 minutes.

Remove the cookies from the oven, then transfer to a wire rack and let them cool completely before serving.

chocolate & brazil nut crunchies

very easy

makes 30 cookies

15 minutes

15 minutes

ingredients

¼ cup butter or margarine,
   plus extra for greasing

¼ cup shortening

scant ¾ cup raw brown sugar

1 egg

1 tsp vanilla extract

1 tbsp milk

⅔ cup all-purpose flour, unsifted

1⅓ cups rolled oats

1 tsp baking soda

pinch of salt

1 cup semisweet chocolate chips

½ cup Brazil nuts, chopped

Preheat the oven to 350°F/180°C. Grease a large cookie sheet.

Put the butter (or margarine, if using), shortening, sugar, egg, vanilla extract and milk in a food processor and blend for at least 3 minutes, or until a fluffy consistency is reached.

In a large bowl, combine the flour, oats, baking soda, and salt. Stir in the egg mixture, then the chocolate chips and Brazil nuts, and mix together thoroughly. Cover the bowl with plastic wrap, and chill in the refrigerator for 30 minutes until the dough is firm.

Put 30 rounded tablespoonfuls of the dough onto the greased cookie sheet, ensuring they are well spaced. Transfer to the oven and bake for 15 minutes, or until the cookies are golden brown.

Remove the cookies from the oven, then transfer to a wire rack and let them cool before serving.

chocolate peanut butter cookies

very easy

makes 24 cookies

10 minutes + 1 hour to chill

20 minutes

ingredients

1 cup butter or margarine, plus extra for greasing
generous 1⅓ cups soft brown sugar
1½ cups coarse peanut butter
1 egg

2 tsp almond extract
2 cups all-purpose flour
1 tsp baking soda
½ cup semisweet chocolate chips
scant ⅔ cup peanuts, chopped

Grease a large cookie sheet. Cream the butter (or margarine) and sugar in a bowl together until fluffy. Add the peanut butter, egg, and almond extract and mix thoroughly.

In a separate bowl, fold in the flour and baking soda; add gradually to the peanut butter mixture. Stir in the chocolate chips and peanuts and mix thoroughly. Cover the bowl with plastic wrap and chill in the refrigerator for 1 hour, or until the dough is firm.

Preheat the oven to 350°F/180°C. Put 24 rounded balls of the dough onto the greased cookie sheet, then flatten with a rolling pin. Ensure that they are well spaced because they may expand during cooking. Transfer to the preheated oven and bake for 20 minutes, or until the cookies are golden brown.

Remove the cookies from the oven, then transfer to a wire rack and let them cool before serving.

chocolate temptations

easy

makes 24
cookies

15–20
minutes

16 minutes

ingredients

12½ oz/365 g semisweet chocolate
6 tbsp unsalted butter, plus extra
   for greasing
1 tsp strong coffee
2 eggs
scant ¾ cup soft brown sugar
generous 1⅓ cups all-purpose flour

¼ tsp baking powder
pinch of salt
2 tsp almond extract
scant ⅔ cup Brazil nuts, chopped
scant ⅔ cup hazelnuts, chopped
1½ oz/40 g white chocolate

Preheat the oven to 350°F/180°C. Grease a large cookie sheet. Put 8 oz/225 g of
the semisweet chocolate with the butter and coffee into a heatproof bowl over a
pan of simmering water and heat until the chocolate is almost melted.

Meanwhile, beat the eggs in a bowl until fluffy. Whisk in the sugar gradually until
thick. Remove the chocolate from the heat and stir until smooth. Stir it into the egg
mixture until combined.

Sift the flour, baking powder, and salt into a bowl and stir into the chocolate
mixture. Chop 3 oz/85 g of semisweet chocolate into pieces and stir into the
dough. Stir in the almond extract and nuts.

Put 24 rounded dessertspoonfuls of the dough onto the cookie sheet and bake for
16 minutes. Transfer the cookies to a wire rack to cool. To decorate, melt the
remaining chocolate (semisweet and white) in turn, then spoon into a piping bag
and pipe lines onto the cookies.

pecan brownies

very easy   makes 20 cookies

15 minutes   30 minutes

ingredients

2½ oz/70 g semisweet chocolate

scant 1 cup all-purpose flour

¾ tsp baking soda

¼ tsp baking powder

1 cup unsalted butter,
  plus extra for greasing

½ cup raw brown sugar

½ tsp almond extract

1 egg

1 tsp milk

⅓ cup pecan nuts, chopped finely

Preheat the oven to 350°F/180°C. Grease a large cookie sheet and line it with baking parchment.

Put the chocolate in a heatproof bowl over a pan of simmering water (a double boiler is ideal) and heat until it is melted. While the chocolate is melting, sift together the flour, baking soda, and baking powder in a large bowl.

In a separate bowl, cream together the butter and sugar, then mix in the almond extract and the egg. Remove the chocolate from the heat and stir into the butter mixture. Add the flour mixture, milk, and chopped nuts to the bowl and stir until well combined.

Spoon the cookie dough onto the greased cookie sheet and level it. Transfer to the preheated oven and cook for 30 minutes, or until firm to the touch (it should still be a little gooey in the middle). Remove from the oven and let cool completely. Cut into 20 squares and serve.

chocolate raisin & almond cookies

ingredients

extremely easy

makes about 56 cookies

15–20 minutes

16 minutes

1 cup butter or margarine,
  plus extra for greasing
2 cups raw brown sugar
2 eggs
1 tsp almond extract
2 cups all-purpose flour, sifted
pinch of salt

1 tsp baking soda
1 tsp baking powder
3 cups rolled oats
generous 2 cups raisins
⅔ cup semisweet chocolate,
  chopped finely
1½ cups almonds, chopped finely

Preheat the oven to 375°F/190°C. Grease a large cookie sheet. Cream the butter and sugar together in a bowl until fluffy. Mix in the eggs and almond extract.

In a separate bowl, sift together the flour, salt, baking soda, and baking powder. Add the egg mixture, along with the rolled oats, raisins, chopped chocolate, and almonds, and mix together thoroughly.

Shape the dough into small balls (about 1 oz/25 g each) and place on the greased cookie sheet, ensuring that they are well spaced. Using a spatula or the bottom of a glass, press the balls down into cookie shapes. Transfer to the preheated oven and bake for 16 minutes, or until the cookies are golden brown.

Remove the cookies from the oven, then transfer to a wire rack and let them cool before serving.

chocolate roundels

extremely easy

makes 24 cookies

20 minutes

10 minutes

ingredients

1 cup butter or margarine,
   plus extra for greasing
1¼ cups raw brown sugar
1 tbsp milk
1 egg
1 tsp almond extract
1 tbsp Amaretto liqueur
1⅔ cups all-purpose flour, sifted,
   plus extra for rolling

1 tsp baking soda
pinch of salt
1 cup semisweet chocolate chips
½ cup hazelnuts, chopped finely
½ cup raisins

confectioners' sugar, to decorate

Preheat the oven to 350°F/180°C. Grease a large cookie sheet. Mix the butter, sugar, and milk together in a bowl. Add the egg, almond extract and Amaretto liqueur and beat well.

In a separate bowl, sift together the flour, baking soda, and salt. Then mix in the egg mixture, along with the chocolate chips, nuts, and raisins. Mix together thoroughly.

Sprinkle flour on a counter or cutting board. Using your hands, roll the dough into balls, then put them onto the greased cookie sheet. Flatten them out into roundels with a rolling pin or the back of a tablespoon. Ensure the roundels are well spaced.

Transfer to the preheated oven and bake for 10 minutes, or until the cookies are golden brown. Transfer to a wire rack and let them cool. Sprinkle over confectioners' sugar before serving.

chocolate & coffee whole-wheat bakes

very easy

makes 24 cookies

10 minutes

16–18 minutes

ingredients

⅜ cup butter or margarine,
   plus extra for greasing
1 cup soft brown sugar
1 egg
½ cup all-purpose flour
1 tsp baking soda
pinch of salt

½ cup whole-wheat flour
1 tbsp bran
1⅓ cups semisweet chocolate chips
generous 2 cups rolled oats
1 tbsp strong coffee
⅔ cup hazelnuts, toasted
   and chopped coarsely

Preheat the oven to 375°F/190°C. Grease a large cookie sheet. Cream the butter and sugar together in a bowl. Add the egg and beat well, using a hand whisk if preferred.

In a separate bowl, sift together the all-purpose flour, baking soda, and salt, then add in the whole-wheat flour and bran. Mix in the egg mixture, then stir in the chocolate chips, oats, coffee, and hazelnuts. Mix well, with an electric hand whisk, if preferred.

Put 24 rounded tablespoonfuls of the dough onto the cookie sheet, ensuring they are well spaced as they expand during cooking. Alternatively, roll the mixture into balls (about 1 oz/25 g each), then place on the cookie sheet and flatten with the back of a teaspoon. Transfer to the preheated oven and bake for 16–18 minutes, or until the cookies are golden brown.

Transfer to a wire rack and let them cool before serving.

white chocolate & apricot cookies

very easy   makes 24 cookies

15 minutes   10 minutes
+ 1 hour
to chill

ingredients

2⅓ cups white chocolate,
    chopped into small pieces
1 cup all-purpose flour, sifted,
    plus extra for dusting
½ tsp baking powder
½ tsp baking soda

pinch of salt
4 tbsp butter, plus extra for greasing
5 tbsp granulated sugar
1 tsp vanilla extract
1 egg
½ cup dried apricots, chopped

Put ½ cup of the white chocolate in a heatproof bowl over a pan of simmering water; stir until melted. Remove from the heat. Sift the flour, baking powder, baking soda, and salt into a separate bowl and mix. In another bowl, cream the butter, sugar, and vanilla. Beat in the egg. Stir in the apricots and chocolate.

Add the dried ingredients and beat well. Using your hands, form the dough into a ball. Cover the bowl with plastic wrap and chill in the refrigerator for at least 1 hour. Preheat the oven to 350°F/180°C. Grease a large cookie sheet.

Roll out the dough into an oblong ¹⁄₁₆ inch/2 mm thick. Cut it into shapes using cookie cutters. Put the shapes on the cookie sheet, then transfer to the oven and bake for 10 minutes. Transfer to a wire rack to cool. Melt the remaining chocolate and dip the cookies in it. Put them upside down on waxed paper and let cool. Store in an airtight container in the refrigerator before serving.

hazelnut bites

extremely
easy

makes 24
cookies

15 minutes

10 minutes

ingredients

½ cup butter,
  plus extra for greasing
¾ cup raw brown sugar
1 egg
1 tbsp almond extract
1 cup all-purpose flour
¾ tsp baking powder

pinch of salt
2 cups rolled oats
½ cup semisweet chocolate chips
⅔ cup hazelnuts, toasted
  and chopped
1¾ cups semisweet chocolate, chopped
  into small pieces

Preheat the oven to 350°F/180°C. Grease a large cookie sheet. Cream the butter and sugar together in a bowl. Add the egg and almond extract and beat well. In a separate bowl, sift together the flour, baking powder, and salt. Beat in the egg mixture. Stir in the oats, chocolate chips, and half of the hazelnuts.

Put 24 rounded tablespoonfuls of the dough onto the cookie sheet and flatten with a rolling pin. Transfer to the preheated oven and bake for 10 minutes, or until the cookies are golden brown.

Remove the cookies from the oven, then transfer to a wire rack and let them cool thoroughly. Put the chocolate pieces in a heatproof bowl over a pan of simmering water and heat until melted. Cover the tops of the cookies with melted chocolate, then top with a sprinkling of the remaining hazelnuts. Let cool on waxed paper. Store in an airtight container in the refrigerator before serving.

From delicately crunchy Orange Horns
to marvelously moist Chewy Golden
Cookies, there is a wide range of
oat-based delights in this section.
Oat cakes are delicious, whether in
their simplest forms, such as Classic
Oatmeal Cookies and Traditional
Spiced Cookies, or combined with nuts,
such as Hazelnut & Almond Oaties,
or with more unusual ingredients to
produce Carrot Cookies or Honeyed
Fig & Walnut Cookies.

oat cookies

classic oatmeal cookies

extremely easy

makes 30 cookies

10 minutes

15 minutes

ingredients

¾ cup butter or margarine,
  plus extra for greasing
scant 1⅓ cups raw brown sugar
1 egg
4 tbsp water

1 tsp vanilla extract
4⅓ cups rolled oats
1 cup all-purpose flour
1 tsp salt
½ tsp baking soda

Preheat the oven to 350°F/180°C and grease a large cookie sheet.

Cream the butter (or margarine, if using) and sugar together in a large mixing bowl. Beat in the egg, water, and vanilla extract until the mixture is smooth.

In a separate bowl, mix the oats, flour, salt, and baking soda. Gradually stir the oat mixture into the butter mixture until thoroughly combined.

Put 30 rounded tablespoonfuls of cookie mixture onto the greased cookie sheet, making sure they are well spaced. Transfer to the preheated oven and bake for 15 minutes, or until the cookies are golden brown.

Remove the cookies from the oven and place on a wire rack to cool before serving.

traditional spiced cookies

extremely easy

makes 36 cookies

15 minutes
+ 1 hour
to chill

12 minutes

ingredients

1½ cups all-purpose flour
2 tsp allspice
1 tsp salt
1 tsp baking soda
¾ cup butter or margarine,
   plus extra for greasing
½ cup granulated sugar

1 cup soft brown sugar,
   plus extra for dusting
2 eggs
4 tbsp milk
3½ cups rolled oats
½ cup raisins
scant ½ cup golden raisins

Mix the flour, allspice, salt, and baking soda together and sift into a large mixing bowl.

One at a time, mix in the butter (or margarine, if using), both sugars, the eggs, and the milk. Beat the mixture until it is smooth.

Add the oats and dried fruit and stir thoroughly. Cover the bowl with plastic wrap and place it in the refrigerator to chill for 1 hour.

Preheat the oven to 375°F/190°C and grease a large cookie sheet.

Put 36 tablespoonfuls of cookie mixture onto the greased cookie sheet, making sure they are well spaced. Dust lightly with soft brown sugar. Transfer to the preheated oven and bake for 12 minutes, or until the cookies are golden brown.

Remove the cookies from the oven and place on a wire rack to cool thoroughly.

hazelnut & almond oaties

extremely easy

makes 36 cookies

10 minutes

12 minutes

ingredients

¼ cup butter or margarine,
   plus extra for greasing

¼ cup raw brown sugar

1 egg

⅔ cup all-purpose flour

½ tsp salt

1 tsp baking soda

¼ tsp almond extract

1½ cups rolled oats

¼ cup hazelnuts, chopped coarsely

¼ cup almonds, chopped coarsely

1 cup semisweet chocolate chips

Preheat the oven to 375°F/190°C and grease a large cookie sheet.

Cream the butter (or margarine, if using) and sugar together in a large mixing bowl. Then beat in the egg.

In a separate bowl, sift the flour, salt, and baking soda, and then stir into the butter mixture.

Add the almond extract and oats and beat thoroughly. Finally, mix in the nuts and chocolate chips.

Put 36 teaspoonfuls of the cookie mixture onto the greased cookie sheet, making sure they are well spaced. Transfer to the oven and bake for 12 minutes, or until the cookies are golden brown.

Remove the cookies from the oven, then place on a wire rack and let them cool before serving.

spiced oat & walnut cookies

extremely
easy

makes 20
cookies

15 minutes

15–20
minutes

ingredients

¼ cup butter or margarine,
   plus extra for greasing
1 cup soft brown sugar
1 cup all-purpose flour
2 tsp baking soda
pinch of salt
1¼ tsp allspice

2 cups rolled oats
2 eggs, beaten
2 tsp vanilla extract
1 cup raisins
1 cup golden raisins
¾ cup walnuts, chopped coarsely

Preheat the oven to 350°F/180°C and grease two large cookie sheets. Cream the butter (or margarine, if using) and sugar together in a large mixing bowl.

In a separate bowl, sift together the flour, baking soda, salt, and allspice, then stir into the butter mixture. Blend in the oats, eggs, and vanilla extract until they are thoroughly combined. Finally, add the dried fruit and nuts and mix well.

Grease a 12½ inch/32 cm x 8½ inch/22 cm jelly pan and cover with baking parchment. Put 48 rounded tablespoonfuls of cookie mixture into the pan, making sure they are well spaced. Transfer to the preheated oven and bake for 20–25 minutes, or until the cookies are firm.

Remove the cookies from the oven and place on a wire rack to cool before serving.

ginger oat cookies

extremely
easy

makes 24
cookies

10 minutes

20–25
minutes

ingredients

¾ cup soft brown sugar

1½ cups all-purpose flour,
    plus extra for dusting

1 cup rolled oats

1 cup bran

½ tsp cinnamon

½ tsp nutmeg

1 tsp ground ginger

½ cup butter or margarine,
    plus extra for greasing

⅔ cup cold water

Preheat the oven to 350°F/180°C and grease a large cookie sheet.

In a large mixing bowl, combine the sugar, flour, oats, bran, and spices. Add the butter (or margarine, if using) and mix with your fingers to make a mixture like bread crumbs. Gradually add the water, continuing to mix with your fingers, until the dough is stiff.

Sprinkle flour onto a cutting board or counter and roll out the dough until it is ½ inch/1 cm thick. Cut into 2 inch/5 cm squares and then place on the cookie sheet.

Transfer to the preheated oven and bake for 20–25 minutes, or until the cookies are golden brown. Remove the cookies from the oven and place on a wire rack to cool before serving.

carrot cookies

extremely easy

makes 24 cookies

10 minutes

12 minutes

ingredients

1 cup all-purpose flour

½ tsp allspice

¼ cup skim milk powder

¼ tsp baking soda

1 tsp baking powder

pinch of salt

4 tbsp butter or margarine,
    plus extra for greasing

scant ⅓ cup soft brown sugar,
    plus extra for dusting

¾ cup corn syrup

1 egg

1 ½ cups carrots, shredded

1 tsp vanilla extract

2 ⅔ cups rolled oats

Preheat the oven to 375°F/190°C and grease a large cookie sheet.

In a medium bowl, sift together the flour, allspice, milk powder, baking soda, baking powder, and salt.

Blend the butter (or margarine, if using), sugar, and corn syrup together in a large bowl. Beat in the egg thoroughly. Add the dry ingredients gradually, stirring continuously. Then blend in the carrots, vanilla extract and oats.

Put 24 tablespoonfuls of cookie mixture onto the cookie sheet, making sure they are well spaced. Dust with soft brown sugar. Transfer to the preheated oven and bake for 12 minutes, or until the cookies are golden brown.

Remove the cookies from the oven, then place on a wire rack and let them cool completely before serving.

oat & hazelnut morsels

extremely easy

makes 30 cookies

10 minutes

12–15 minutes

ingredients

¾ cup butter or margarine,
  plus extra for greasing
1¼ cup raw brown sugar
1 egg, beaten
4 tbsp milk
1 tsp vanilla extract
½ tsp almond extract

1 cup all-purpose flour
1½ tsp allspice
¼ tsp baking soda
pinch of salt
3½ cups rolled oats
scant 1 cup golden raisins
¾ cup hazelnuts, chopped finely

Preheat the oven to 375°F/190°C. Grease 2 large cookie sheets.

Cream the butter (or margarine, if using) and sugar together in a large mixing bowl. Blend in the egg, milk, vanilla extract and almond extract until they are thoroughly combined.

In a separate bowl, sift the all-purpose flour, allspice, baking soda, and salt together thoroughly. Add to the creamed mixture slowly, stirring continuously. Mix in the oats, golden raisins and hazelnuts.

Put 30 rounded tablespoonfuls of cookie mixture onto the greased cookie sheets, making sure they are well spaced. Transfer to the preheated oven and bake for 12–15 minutes, or until the cookies are golden brown.

Remove the cookies from the oven and place on a wire rack to cool before serving.

honeyed fig & walnut cookies

very easy

makes 20 cookies

15 minutes

10–15 minutes

ingredients

1 cup butter or margarine,
   plus extra for greasing

⅓ cup honey

scant ⅓ cup dried figs, chopped finely

¼ cup raw brown sugar

2 eggs, beaten

pinch of salt

1 tsp allspice

1 tsp baking soda

½ tsp vanilla extract

2 tbsp dried dates, chopped finely

1½ cups all-purpose flour

2 cups rolled oats

⅓ cup walnuts, chopped finely

fig pieces, to decorate

Preheat the oven to 350°F/180°C and grease a large cookie sheet.

Mix the butter (or margarine, if using), honey, figs, and sugar together in a large bowl. Beat in the eggs and mix thoroughly.

Combine the salt, allspice, baking soda, vanilla extract and dates, stirring continuously. Add them to the creamed mixture gradually. Sift the flour into the mixture, stirring continuously. Finally, mix in the oats and walnuts.

Drop 20 rounded tablespoonfuls of cookie mixture onto the greased cookie sheet, making sure they are well spaced. Decorate with fig pieces, if desired. Bake in the preheated oven for 10–15 minutes, or until the cookies are golden brown.

Transfer the cookies from the oven to a wire rack and let cool before serving.

orange horns

easy

makes 30
cookies

10 minutes

7 minutes

½ cup butter or margarine,
   plus extra for greasing
⅔ cup soft brown sugar
pinch of salt
1 egg white, beaten lightly
½ tsp baking powder

½ cup oatmeal
1 cup Brazil nuts (or hazelnuts),
   chopped finely
1 tbsp milk
1 tsp orange juice
1 tsp orange zest, grated finely

Preheat the oven to 325°F/160°C and grease a large cookie sheet.

Blend the butter (or margarine, if using) and sugar together in a bowl until the mixture is fluffy. Add the remaining ingredients and mix thoroughly.

Drop 30 rounded teaspoonfuls of the mixture onto the cookie sheet and flatten into small circles using the bottom of a glass. Transfer to the preheated oven and bake for 7 minutes, then remove from the oven.

Let cool slightly. Place each cookie in turn on a rolling pin to help start the desired curve, completing the horn shape by hand, while the cookie is still warm.

Let the cookies cool on a wire rack before serving.

chewy golden cookies

extremely easy   makes 30 cookies

12 minutes   12 minutes

ingredients

¾ cup butter or margarine,
  plus extra for greasing
scant 1½ cups soft brown sugar
1 cup corn syrup
3 egg whites
6 cups rolled oats

2 cups all-purpose flour
pinch of salt
1 tsp baking powder

confectioners' sugar, to drizzle

Preheat the oven to 350°F/180°C and grease a large cookie sheet.

In a large mixing bowl, blend the butter (or margarine, if using), sugar, syrup and egg whites together. Gradually add the oats, flour, salt, and baking powder and mix thoroughly.

Drop 30 rounded tablespoonfuls of the mixture onto the cookie sheet and transfer to the preheated oven.

Bake for 12 minutes, or until the cookies are light brown.

Remove from the oven and let them cool on a wire rack. Drizzle over the confectioners' sugar and serve.

Basic cookie doughs can be completely transformed by the addition of fresh or dried fruit and crunchy, mouthwatering nuts. Here is a selection of cookies that contain bananas, lemons, oranges–Banana Pecan Cookies, Lemon Discs, Orange Cream Cheese Cookies–and an array of nuts–Cherry & Walnut Cookies, Spiced Almond Cookies, and Mixed Nut Cookies.

fruit & nut cookies

banana pecan cookies

extremely
easy

makes 20
cookies

12 minutes

15 minutes

⅔ cup butter or margarine,
　plus extra for greasing
⅔ cup soft brown sugar
1 egg
1½ cups all-purpose flour
1 tbsp baking powder
¼ tsp baking soda

pinch of salt
2 tsp allspice
4 tbsp milk
1 cup mashed bananas
3 cups rolled oats
⅔ cup pecan nuts,
　toasted and chopped coarsely

Preheat the oven to 375°F/190°C. Grease a large cookie sheet. Cream the butter and sugar in a large mixing bowl, then beat in the egg.

Gradually sift the flour, baking powder, baking soda, salt, and allspice into the creamed mixture and mix thoroughly. Stir in the 4 tablespoons of milk and the mashed banana. Finally, add the oats and chopped pecan nuts and mix well.

Drop 20 rounded tablespoonfuls of the dough onto the greased cookie sheet, ensuring that they are well spaced. Transfer to the preheated oven and bake for 15 minutes, or until the cookies are light brown.

Transfer from the oven to a wire rack and let them cool completely before serving.

fruit morsels

extremely easy

makes 36 cookies

12 minutes

10 minutes

ingredients

1 cup all-purpose flour

scant 1 cup rolled oats

1 cup wheat flakes

½ tsp baking soda

pinch of salt

¾ cup soft brown sugar,
plus extra for dusting

½ cup butter or margarine,
plus extra for greasing

2 eggs

1 tsp almond extract

1 cup chopped dried apricots

½ cup chopped dried dates

Preheat the oven to 375°F/190°C.

Sift the flour into a large bowl and mix in the oats, wheat flakes, baking soda and salt.

Blend the sugar and butter (or margarine, if using). Beat in the eggs until the mixture is light and fluffy. Add the flour mixture gradually, stirring continuously. Then blend in the almond extract and dried fruit. Mix thoroughly.

Drop 36 teaspoonfuls of cookie mixture onto a large greased cookie sheet, making sure they are well spaced. Dust with soft brown sugar. Transfer to the preheated oven and bake for 10 minutes, or until the cookies are golden brown.

Remove the cookies from the oven, place on a wire rack and let them cool before serving.

spiced fruit & nut cookies

extremely easy

makes 20 cookies

12 minutes

20 minutes

ingredients

1⅓ cups mashed bananas

⅓ cup vegetable oil

1 tsp almond extract

1 egg, beaten

1 tsp allspice

pinch of salt

3 cups rolled oats

½ cup raisins

scant ½ cup golden raisins

½ cup dates, chopped finely

⅓ cup walnuts, chopped finely

Preheat the oven to 350°F/180°C and grease a large cookie sheet.

Blend the bananas, oil, almond extract, egg, allspice, and salt together in a large mixing bowl. Add the oats and mix well. Finally, stir in the dried fruit and walnuts until evenly distributed.

Drop 20 rounded tablespoonfuls of cookie mixture onto the greased cookie sheet, making sure they are well spaced.

Bake in the preheated oven for 20 minutes, or until the cookies are golden brown.

Transfer the cookies from the oven to a wire rack and let them cool completely before serving.

caribbean cookies

extremely easy

makes 24 cookies

12 minutes

10 minutes

ingredients

¼ cup mashed banana
1 tbsp pineapple juice
1 tbsp orange juice
¼ cup peanut oil
1 egg
1 tbsp milk

1 cup all-purpose flour
¼ tsp baking soda
¾ cup dry, unsweetened coconut

raw brown sugar, to sprinkle

Preheat the oven to 350°F/180°C. Grease a large cookie sheet.

In a large mixing bowl, cream together the banana, fruit juices, oil, egg and milk.

Sift in the flour and baking soda gradually, stirring continuously. Stir in the coconut and mix well.

Drop rounded teaspoonfuls onto the greased cookie sheet, making sure that they are well spaced. Sprinkle with the raw brown sugar. Transfer to the preheated oven and bake for 10 minutes, or until the cookies are golden brown.

Remove the cookies from the oven and transfer to a wire rack to cool before serving.

cherry & walnut cookies

very easy   makes 30 cookies

12 minutes   10 minutes

¾ cup butter or margarine,
  plus extra for greasing
1 cup soft brown sugar
2 eggs
2¼ cups all-purpose flour
pinch of salt
2 tsp baking powder
2 tbsp milk
1 tsp almond extract

1 cup chopped walnuts
½ cup raisins
scant ½ cup golden raisins
½ cup maraschino cherries
2 cups wheat flakes, crushed

15 maraschino cherries, cut in half
  (optional)

Preheat the oven to 375°F/190°C. Grease a large cookie sheet.

Cream the butter and sugar in a large mixing bowl until a fluffy consistency is reached. Beat in the eggs.

Gradually sift the flour, salt, and baking powder into the creamed mixture. Add the milk and almond extract and mix thoroughly. Stir in the walnuts and dried fruit and mix well.

Form the dough into 30 balls (about 1 rounded tablespoon each) and roll in the crushed wheat flakes. Space the dough balls about 1 inch/2 cm apart on the greased cookie sheet. Place half a maraschino cherry on the top of each dough ball, if desired. Transfer to the preheated oven and cook for 10 minutes, or until the cookies are light brown.

Transfer from the oven to a wire rack and let them cool.

lemon disks

extremely
easy

makes
30 cookies

15 minutes

10 minutes

ingredients

¾ cup butter or margarine,
   plus extra for greasing
1 cup soft brown sugar,
   plus extra for dusting
2 tbsp corn syrup
1 egg
2½ cups all-purpose flour
pinch of salt

1 tsp baking soda
1 tsp ground ginger
1 tsp allspice
1 tsp grated lemon zest

raw brown sugar, for dusting

ground cinnamon, to decorate

Preheat the oven to 375°F/190°C. Grease a large cookie sheet.

Cream the butter or margarine (if using), sugar, and corn syrup in a large mixing bowl. Beat in the egg.

Gradually sift the flour, salt, baking soda, ginger and allspice into the creamed mixture, stirring continuously. Add the lemon zest and mix thoroughly.

Form the dough into 30 or so balls (about 1 rounded tablespoon each). Space the dough balls about 1 inch/2 cm apart on the greased cookie sheet and flatten slightly with a spatula. Dust the dough balls with raw brown sugar. Transfer to the preheated oven and cook for 10 minutes, or until the cookies are light brown.

Transfer from the oven to a wire rack and let them cool completely. Sprinkle with cinnamon and serve.

orange cream cheese cookies

very easy   makes 30 cookies

15 minutes   10 minutes

1 cup butter or margarine,
  plus extra for greasing
1 cup soft brown sugar
6 tbsp cream cheese
1 egg, beaten lightly
2⅓ cups all-purpose flour

1 tsp baking soda
1 tbsp orange juice
1 tsp finely grated orange zest

raw brown sugar, to sprinkle

Preheat the oven to 375°F/190°C. Grease a large cookie sheet.

In a large mixing bowl, cream together the butter (or margarine, if using), sugar, and cream cheese until light and fluffy. Mix in the egg and sift in the flour and baking soda. Add the orange juice and zest and mix well.

Drop about 30 rounded tablespoonfuls onto the greased cookie sheet, making sure that they are well spaced. Sprinkle with the raw brown sugar.

Transfer to the preheated oven and bake for 10 minutes, or until the cookies are light brown at the edges.

Remove the cookies from the oven and let them cool on a wire rack before serving.

spiced almond cookies

extremely easy

makes 30 cookies

12 minutes
+30 minutes
to chill

15 minutes

ingredients

¾ cup butter or margarine,
   plus extra for greasing
½ cup superfine sugar
scant ¼ cup almonds, chopped finely
½ tsp allspice
pinch of salt
1 tsp vanilla extract

1⅔ cups all-purpose flour
1 egg white, beaten lightly

chopped almonds, to decorate

Preheat the oven to 325°F/160°C and grease 2 large cookie sheets. Mix half the sugar with the chopped almonds and allspice and set aside.

In a mixing bowl, cream the butter (or margarine, if using) and half the sugar with the salt and vanilla extract. Sift in the flour and mix well. Cover the bowl with plastic wrap and transfer to the refrigerator to chill for 30 minutes.

Sprinkle flour on a counter or cutting board and roll out the dough to ½ inch/1 cm thickness. Using a pastry cutter or glass, cut the dough into circles 2 inches/5 cm in diameter. Transfer to the cookie sheets. Brush lightly with egg white and prick with a fork.

Sprinkle with the sugar and almond mixture. Transfer to the oven and bake for 15 minutes, or until the cookies are golden. Remove from the oven and sprinkle with chopped almonds before serving.

mixed nut cookies

very easy

makes 36 cookies

12 minutes

12–14 minutes

ingredients

½ cup butter or margarine,
  plus extra for greasing
½ cup superfine sugar
½ cup soft brown sugar
pinch of salt
1 tsp almond extract
2 egg whites, beaten lightly

3 tsp water
1 cup all-purpose flour
½ tsp baking powder
½ tsp baking soda
2 cups rolled oats
scant ¼ cup mixed nuts,
  chopped finely

Preheat the oven to 375°F/190°C. Grease 2 large cookie sheets.

In a large mixing bowl, cream the butter (or margarine, if using), sugars, salt and almond extract until the mixture is light and fluffy. Beat in the egg whites and water. Sift in the flour, baking powder, and baking soda and mix well. Finally, blend in the oats and mixed nuts until evenly distributed.

Drop 36 rounded tablespoons of the dough onto the cookie sheets. Transfer to the oven and bake for 12–14 minutes.

Remove from the oven and transfer to a wire rack to cool completely before serving.

Sweet treats are a traditional feature of many kinds of special occasions, from birthdays to St. Valentine's Day to Christmas. Why not cheer up a children's party with some Snowy Chocolate Crispies or add a little pep to a more grown-up gathering with some Banana Brandies? Of course, you don't have to wait for someone's birthday to try out the treats in the next few pages. Every day is cause for celebration when you have tempting festive cookies on the table.

festive cookies

banana brandies

easy   makes 20 cookies

15 minutes   20–25 minutes

scant 1 cup all-purpose flour
1 tsp baking powder
pinch of salt
1 tsp allspice
1½ bananas, chopped coarsely
¾ cup apple purée
1 tsp brandy

¾ cup corn syrup
generous 1 cup rolled oats
2 tbsp golden raisins

DECORATION
1 tbsp chopped candied mixed fruit
1 tbsp chopped dried banana chips

Preheat the oven to 350°F/180°C. Grease a large cookie sheet. Sift together the flour, baking powder, salt, and allspice into a large bowl.

Put the fresh banana pieces, apple purée, brandy, and corn syrup in a food processor and blend together until smooth. Stir in the oats and golden raisins. Add the banana mixture to the spiced flour and mix together thoroughly.

Put 20 rounded tablespoonfuls of the cookie mixture onto the greased cookie sheet, making sure that they are well spaced in case they expand during cooking. Transfer to the preheated oven and bake for 20–25 minutes, or until golden brown.

Remove the cookies from the oven and place on a wire rack to cool. Before serving, decorate with the chopped candied mixed fruit and the banana chips.

jamaican rum cookies

easy   makes 36 cookies

15 minutes   8 minutes

ingredients

¾ cup butter or margarine,
   plus extra for greasing
⅓ cup sesame seeds
generous ⅓ cup chopped mixed nuts
1 cup all-purpose flour
¼ tsp baking powder
pinch of salt

1½ cups raw brown sugar
1 egg
1 tsp spiced rum

2 tbsp sweet coconut flakes,
   to decorate

Preheat the oven to 350°F/180°C. Grease a large cookie sheet.

Spread the sesame seeds and chopped nuts out on an ungreased cookie sheet and toast them for about 10 minutes, or until slightly browned. Remove from the oven and set aside. Leave the oven on.

Sift together the flour, baking powder, and salt in a large mixing bowl. Add the sugar, egg, and spiced rum and beat together well.

Put 36 rounded teaspoonfuls of the mixture onto the greased cookie sheet. Make sure they are well spaced in case they expand during baking. Transfer to the preheated oven and bake for about 8 minutes, or until golden brown.

Remove from the oven and set aside to cool on a wire rack. Decorate with the coconut flakes and serve.

snowy chocolate crispies

extremely
easy

makes 24
cookies

10 minutes

10 minutes
to set

ingredients

1 cup butter
generous ½ cup corn syrup
1⅓ cups semisweet chocolate,
    chopped into small pieces
2 cups toasted rice cereal
1⅓ cups white chocolate,
    chopped into small pieces

In a small pan, gently warm the butter and corn syrup over a low heat, until the butter has dissolved. Stir in the chopped semisweet chocolate until it has melted.

Remove from the heat and add the toasted rice cereal. Stir thoroughly to ensure the rice is evenly coated. Spoon the mixture into 24 fairy cake cases and set aside to set for 5 minutes.

Meanwhile, put the white chocolate pieces in a heatproof bowl over a pan of simmering water and heat until melted. Pour a teaspoonful of melted chocolate on top of each crispie cake and put aside to set for 10 minutes before serving.

gingerbread squares

easy · makes 24 cookies

10 minutes · 10 minutes

6 tbsp butter or margarine,
   plus extra for greasing
¼ cup soft brown sugar
5 tbsp molasses
1 egg white
1 tsp almond extract
scant 1½ cups all-purpose flour,
   plus extra for dusting

¼ tsp baking soda
¼ tsp baking powder
pinch of salt
½ tsp allspice
½ tsp ground ginger
scant ½ cup dessert apples,
   cooked and chopped finely

Preheat the oven to 180°C/350°F. Grease a large cake pan and line it with baking parchment. Put the butter (or margarine, if using), sugar, molasses, egg white, and almond extract in a food processor and blend until smooth.

In a separate bowl, sift together the flour, baking soda, baking powder, salt, allspice, and ginger. Add to the creamed mixture and beat together thoroughly. Stir in the chopped apples. Pour the mixture into the lined cake pan.

Transfer to the preheated oven and bake for 10 minutes, or until golden brown. Remove from the oven and cut into 24 pieces. Transfer the cookies to a wire rack and let them cool completely before serving.

yuletide cookies

very easy

makes 24 cookies

20 minutes + 4 hours to chill

10 minutes

ingredients

7 cups all-purpose flour,
plus extra for dusting
1 tbsp baking soda
1 tbsp powdered ginger
3 tsp allspice
pinch of salt
1 cup butter or margarine,
plus extra for greasing

1½ cups corn syrup
1 cup raw brown sugar
½ cup water
1 egg
1 tsp brandy
1 tsp very finely grated orange zest

confectioners' sugar, to decorate

In a large bowl, sift together the flour, baking soda, ginger, allspice, and salt. In a separate bowl, beat together the butter (or margarine, if using), corn syrup, sugar, water, egg, and brandy until thoroughly combined. Gradually stir in the grated orange zest, then the flour mixture.

Halve the dough, then wrap in plastic wrap and refrigerate for at least 4 hours (it will keep for up to 6 days). When ready to use, preheat the oven to 350°F/180°C and grease a cookie sheet.

Flour a board or counter. Roll each half of dough into a ball, then roll it to a thickness of ⅛ inch/3 mm. Using cookie cutters or a knife, cut festive shapes such as stars and trees. Put the cookies onto the cookie sheet, then transfer to the oven and bake for 10 minutes, or until golden brown. Remove the cookies from the oven and transfer to a wire rack, then set aside. When the cookies have cooled, drizzle over the confectioners' sugar and serve.

cheese & peanut crescents

very easy

makes 24
cookies

10 minutes
+ 2 hours
to chill

15 minutes

ingredients

3 cups all-purpose flour,
   plus extra for dusting
pinch of salt
1 cup peanut butter
4 cups hard cheese (eg Cheddar),
   finely grated
1¼ cups butter or margarine,
   plus extra for greasing
1 tsp almond extract

DECORATION
mixed nuts, toasted and chopped coarsely
confectioners' sugar

In a large bowl, sift together the flour and salt. Add the peanut butter, cheese, butter (or margarine, if using), and almond extract. Mix together until thoroughly combined, then cover with plastic wrap and refrigerate for 2 hours.

Preheat the oven to 350°F/180°C. Grease a large cookie sheet. Lightly flour a board or work surface. Cut the dough into 24 small pieces and, using your hands, roll each piece into a ball about 1 inch/2.5 cm in diameter. Then roll out each ball into a circle about ⅛ inch/3 mm in thickness. Using a knife, cut a crescent moon out of each circle by removing about one fourth of the dough from each one. Put the crescents onto the cookie sheet, then transfer to the oven and bake for 15 minutes, or until golden brown.

Remove the cookies from the oven and transfer to a wire rack, then sprinkle over the nuts and confectioners' sugar and set aside to cool.

melting hearts

extremely easy

makes 24 cookies

10 minutes + 8 hours to chill

15 minutes

ingredients

1 cups all-purpose flour, plus extra for dusting

1½ tsp allspice

½ tsp powdered ginger

pinch of salt

½ tsp baking soda

½ cup butter or margarine, plus extra for greasing

½ cup soft brown sugar

2 small eggs

1 tsp cocoa powder

½ tsp Kahlua liqueur

¾ cup hazelnuts, toasted and chopped coarsely

½ cup heavy cream or crème fraîche, to serve

12 fresh mint leaves, to decorate

In a large bowl, sift together the flour, spices, salt, and baking soda. In a separate bowl, cream together the butter (or margarine, if using) and sugar. Beat in the eggs, then add the cocoa powder, Kahlua, and flour mixture gradually and continue beating until smooth. Cover with plastic wrap and refrigerate for at least 8 hours or overnight if possible.

When ready to use, preheat the oven to 350°F/180°C and grease a cookie sheet. Lightly flour a board or counter. Roll out the dough into an oblong about ⅛ in/3 mm thick, then cut out 24 heart shapes using a cookie cutter or a sharp knife. Place the hearts onto the greased cookie sheet. Transfer to the oven and bake for 15 minutes, or until the cookies are golden brown.

Remove from the oven, then transfer to a wire rack and sprinkle over the hazelnuts. When cool, serve with cream or crème fraîche topped with fresh mint leaves.

sugared orange diamonds

extremely
easy

makes 24
cookies

10 minutes
+ 2 hours
to chill

15 minutes

ingredients

½ cup butter or margarine,
   plus extra for greasing
¾ cup raw brown sugar
2 tbsp orange juice
1 tbsp Cointreau liqueur
2½ cups all-purpose flour, sifted,
   plus extra for dusting

1½ cups walnuts, chopped coarsely
1 tbsp finely grated orange zest

confectioners' sugar, to decorate

Put the butter, sugar, orange juice, and Cointreau in a bowl and beat together until
a fluffy consistency is reached.

In a separate bowl, mix together the flour, walnuts, and orange zest. Add the butter
mixture and mix until thoroughly combined. Cover with plastic wrap and chill in
the refrigerator for 2 hours.

When ready to use, preheat the oven to 350°F/180°C. Grease a large cookie sheet.

Lightly flour a board or counter. Roll out the dough into an oblong about
⅛ in/3 mm thick, then use a sharp knife or cookie cutter to cut out 24 diamonds.
Put the diamonds onto the greased cookie sheet. Transfer to the oven and bake for
15 minutes, or until the cookies are golden brown.

Remove the cookies from the oven, transfer to a wire rack and let them cool.
Decorate with confectioners' sugar before serving.

lemon drops

very easy   makes 24
             cookies

10 minutes   10 minutes

ingredients

½ cup butter or margarine,
   plus extra for greasing
1 cup superfine sugar
2 tbsp lemon juice
1 tbsp finely grated lemon zest
2 tbsp water
1½ cups all-purpose flour, sifted

1 tsp baking soda
½ tsp cream of tartar

DECORATION
confectioners' sugar
candied mixed fruit, chopped finely
   (optional)

Preheat the oven to 350°F/180°C. Grease a large cookie sheet. Beat together the butter, superfine sugar, lemon juice, lemon zest, and water.

In a separate bowl, mix together the flour, baking soda, and cream of tartar. Add the butter mixture and blend well.

Spoon the mixture into a piping bag fitted with a star-shaped nozzle. Pipe 24 fancy drops, about the size of a tablespoon, onto the greased cookie sheet, ensuring that they are well spaced because they may expand during cooking. Transfer to the preheated oven and bake for 10 minutes, or until the lemon drops are golden brown.

Remove the cookies from the oven, then transfer to a wire rack and let them cool completely. When ready to serve, dust with confectioners' sugar and sprinkle over the candied fruit, if desired.

index